Borne

Abigail Lovell

Presentation by *BookLeaf Publishing*

Web: www.bookleafpub.com

E-mail: info@bookleafpub.com

ISBN: 9789357440714

First edition 2023

For Elliot, my bright-eyed boy

and

for Thea, my littlest love

ACKNOWLEDGEMENT

To Samuel, for all the encouragement and patience as I worried, wrote, and re-wrote.

To our families, church family and friends who prayed with and for us, supported us in so many different ways, and continue to love us even when we are at our least loveable.

Thank you.

PREFACE

When I first thought of the title for this poetry collection and the themes it brought with it, I hesitated. But it was my hesitation that became a motivation, in the end. Words have often failed me in the incoherence of grief and silence tends to surround a subject as shocking as miscarriage and baby loss, and I wondered whether anyone else had felt the lonely weight of that silence.

Whilst I cannot make any claim to represent anything beyond my own experience, my hope was to try to share something of what happened, to put a little book out into the world that gives voice an often untold story and honours a life never lived.

September

Does autumn always feel this heavy?
Thighs, stomach, arms - my body -
Silent and somnolent,
Aching with its own weight
In a morning.

These days I am very bodied,
Aware of every creak
And the thud of my feet
Solid when they meet
The floor.

Morning half-light rises, splutters
And I wonder, groggily,
Is waking any less murky
Than crunchy-eyed dreaming?
Time swims on.

Sometimes there is a brightness
In the crisp air, even still.
The edges of my days ring
With structured beat, echoing
Academic diaries.

And so September's music tugs at
My body - Arms, stomach, thighs -
Thin, keen notes of silver,
Glinting with the start
Of something.

Arrival

In this place of chaotic heat
The air is sweet
With milky exhalations,
And swimming with the stamp
Of muddled feet.

Small starfish hands latch.
Curling, they catch
In the unbrushed net of my hair.
Seeking to entangle and
Never detach.

I feel my edges, softly frayed skin,
I am wearing thin.
And it's hard to decipher
Where I must end
And where you begin.

Your knitted hat

3

Tiny dot of red
Drawing my sandpaper gaze
Inevitably.

They tell me to sleep
When he is sleeping and I
Fight the urge to laugh,
Eyes transfixed by vermilion,
Exhausted by joy.

Elastic

See me stretching,
My patience pulled here and there,
Worn at the elbows.
Clothes that used to drape
Straining tighter with each wear,
As silver marks grow.

Lack of rest tugs
At the dark circles that seep
Below my dry eyes.
I am bound tight by
Taut strings that haul me from sleep
At sound of keen cries.

Waiting

When the cherry tumbles apart at the seams
And blossom, confetti like, falls swift and slow,
Anticipation rises to stretch strong wing,
And weaves a bold path amidst soft ebb and flow.

The whisper-soft weight of our purposeful dreams
Treads a track through petals that no longer grow.
March seems a good time to ponder new things;
A future which slumbers in dappled shadow.

Beat

One small cough,
Clearing of a cluttered throat,
And we are floored.

Scrape us up,
Separate out the pieces,
And pour us back
Into chairs
That cannot stand the thunder
Of our heartbeats.

Square, white room.
I want to colour the walls
With my questions
But they lodge
Intractable, silenced by
My racing pulse.

All the while
The sound of the foetal doppler,
Against all odds,
Echoes on,
Proclaiming, if they'll listen
That, still, you -are-.

Snapshot

7

We picnic on hot tarmac,
Hands sticky with a slight film of sweat and dust,
Grasping at straws to sip from flattened coke.
Over a red carseat, our red eyes meet,
And hope waltzes hand-in-hand with heartbreak.
Between us, pink-cheeked joy looks up and bright eyes
Open wide, let in the sky.

10.06.21

Time after time,
We traced the lines,
Your delicate frame;
Head, shoulders, spine.
With inexpert eyes,
We strained to see sign
Of your fragile heart beating,
Much faster than mine.

Scan after scan,
In rooms white and bland,
I'd lie transfixed
By the wave of small hand.
My own heart beat fast
With future unplanned
But there was a strange beauty
In this no-man's land.

Day after day,
Hard to overstate
The simple strangeness
Of this bittersweet wait.
Time's changeable pace
Seemed not to abate
But swift, marched us on
Toward this precious date.

Boulversé

9

I call from this now familiar room,
White walls sucking at my understanding.
There cannot be a good way to share this,
So I know that I will mangle the news,
Horror hovering in the soft tremor
Of hello.

There would usually be some amusement
In crossing wires, the tragicomedy
Of absurd attempts to make ourselves heard,
Of hanging up and using the landline,
Fingers mashing the wrong keys, wondering
If you know.

You must have known. Surely the very earth
Had ceased spinning, stuttered on its axis
In that one stretching moment of silence.
My mother, so entranced by the beauty
Of delicate frame, had suddenly seen
The stillness.

What is there to do but go on our way
To the car and the strangest, saddest wait?
My body, a walking coffin and yet
Still curling protective, around treasure.
In the heat, I shake my fist at the sun
For shining.

Back home, the light blazes in through curtains,
Welcome or not, it will keep on rising.
Encircled in arms that hold us upright
With a myriad of small kindnesses,
We trip over days that bring us closer
To goodbye.

Exit

We leave at 5 minutes past midnight.
There is something furtive at this hour,
Despite the glare of baleful lights
My mouth feels arid, acrid, sour.

Did they delay our discharge
So that our empty arms and hands
Wouldn't disturb the ward with grief too large
For our brittle bodies to withstand?

There never was real rest here.
In a bare, box room, exhaustion reigned,
But my torn heart, stubborn mutineer,
Pulls me to a stop, all energy drained.

I am rooted to the spot, legs overthrown,
Cannot stand the weight of goodbye,
But know that to endlessly postpone
Would not dry my tear-drenched eyes.

Beyond this place, I don't know how,
We'll stumble on, our arms enlaced,
Remembering that now, somehow,
This life goes on, still to be faced.

Wreath

I make the wreath,
Weave tiny daisies
And carnations, slightly faded
Amongst rosemary still misty
With dew from the garden.

I concentrate,
Welcome the sharp cold
Of metal twine which winds
Around my shaking fingers
Gradually taking shape.

Finished, I wait,
Surrounded by stray leaves
While the pale smallness
Of this fragile circle
Takes my breath away.

Goodnight

Where waters fall and rowan grows,
Sound is shrouded in green shadows,
And footfalls land with no echoes.

Our quiet words seem out of place,
Where fronds of emerald interlace.
Creation sings the Father's grace.

Oh would that we were here as four,
To cross this brook, jump shore to shore
With untold future still in store.

Instead, forlorn hands clasping tight,
We lean, statues, in dappled light,
Prepare for this: our last goodnight.

'How are you?'

13

I appreciate
You asking, but answering
Is complicated.

When I say 'I'm fine,'
I do not mean to shut down
The conversation.

But how to convey
The weight of this new normal
Without a cliché?

Whatever I say,
Behind my words, there hovers
A silence, as yet unheard.

Phatic

I used to navigate these simple seas with ease.
The light eddies of small talk swirling naturally.

But now I am out of my depth in a puddle,
Muddling along with a rudder that struggles.

Swiftly saturated, I am perforated,
Cradling this conversation with my fingers splayed.

Words run. Her name is a rock tethered to my tongue.
Air from my lungs blunders past and I come undone.

Grief speaks
.
A tsunami of silence ripples out leaving me
Beached.

Vacuum

15

You'd think that writing
Would come naturally.
After all, I am filled
With an estuary of words.
They dissolve into a
Cacophony of language,
Combining to create
A crowded sea of
Silence.

Often I scream
These words into the air,
Painting wild shapes
Across the livid sky
Of my mind: an empty world
Full of you.

Editing

I censor myself often.
Should I polish and soften?
And is it too shocking
To write 'walking coffin'?

I don't dream of the hospital

I don't dream of the hospital.
I dream endlessly of the search for a parking space.
The hurried bundling of my heavy self out of what felt like a
still-moving car.
In the night, roads twist dangerously vertical,
Then jerk round to flatten out again,
Before swivelling, tipping the car on its head.
I have fallen over and over,
And over.

I don't dream of the hospital.
I dream of unnumbered phone calls.
Explaining the unspeakable, ripping open the truth
With words that attempt calm fact.
My skin ripples like an old black and white movie.
Turbulent surface contained in an egg cup -
It has brimmed over and over,
And over.

I don't dream of the hospital.
I dream of fields of yellow poppies glowing golden
Swayed to and fro by caressing warmth of jewel-bright breezes.
Of a small figure in far corner, face turned to the horizon.
I do not presume to call this prophecy or revelation, but know
One day, in perfected eternity, I'll catch you up, tell you
I love you, over and over,
And over.

Twisted

They say that grief is love
Turned inside out.

But it feels like it has turned me
Upside down and back to front
As well.

Love has kept us

Swept us off our feet in the light brightness of romance,
Danced us hand in hand through promises of forever,
Settled us comfortably into familiar routines,
Etched our hearts with the urgent tug of parenthood,
Hurt us and held us in wretched brokenness,
And showed us hope to be found in the One who is love.

Yellow Coat

The sky is ice-hued
And storm clouds brood.
From twisting trees,
Dark bones protrude.

It is winter here.

Underfoot, stones click.
Snow does not stick,
But fast-falling flakes
Make pavements slick.

Your yellow coat glows,
Short flurry slows,
You scurry ahead
Through grey shadows.

The wind is bitter.

I'm gripped by sharp fright
That I'll lose sight
Of darting figure
In swift-falling night.

I race to catch up.

Oh little boy, with all my love,
I want to lift you up above,
To place this yellow coat so high,
That shadows do not catch your eye,
Protect you from my visioned fears,
Pre-empt, prevent your every tear.
But this is not within my gift,
And so I merely come and lift
You in my arms to take you home,
Safe 'til the next time that we roam.

Inside, it is warm.

Abstract

They say that love is just an abstract noun
But I've found that the dictionary knows less about it
Than we do.